Lightning Bolt Books™

Real-Life Ninja

Jon M. Fishman

Lerner Publications ◆ Minneapolis

Lerner Publications Company
An imprint of Lerner Publishing Group, Inc.
241 First Avenue North
Minneapolis, MN 55401 USA

For reading levels and more information, look up this title at www.lernerbooks.com.

Library of Congress Cataloging-in-Publication Data

Names: Fishman, Jon M., author.
Title: Real-life ninja / Jon M. Fishman.
Description: Minneapolis : Lerner Publications, [2020] | Series: Lightning bolt books : ninja mania | Includes bibliographical references and index. | Audience: Ages: 6-9 | Audience: Grades: 2-3 | Summary: "A figure clothed in black scales a castle wall for a covert mission. But how did ninja actually live their lives? Uncover the secrets and truth of living life as a ninja"— Provided by publisher.
Identifiers: LCCN 2019028066 (print) | LCCN 2019028067 (ebook) | ISBN 9781541577060 (library binding) | ISBN 9781541589186 (paperback) | ISBN 9781541583276 (ebook)
Subjects: LCSH: Ninja—Juvenile literature. | Ninjutsu—Juvenile literature. | Ninja—Japan—Juvenile literature. | Japan—History, Military—To 1868—Juvenile literature.
Classification: LCC UB271.J3 F572 2020 (print) | LCC UB271.J3 (ebook) | DDC 355.5/48—dc23

LC record available at https://lccn.loc.gov/2019028066
LC ebook record available at https://lccn.loc.gov/2019028067

Manufactured in the United States of America
1-46728-47719-8/26/2019

Table of Contents

Secret Soldiers 4
Ninja Tales 8
Ninja in Action 12
Modern Ninja 16
Real-Life Ninja 20
Ninja Fun Facts 21
Glossary 22
Further Reading 23
Index 24

Secret Soldiers

A ninja walks quietly through a dark field. She hides and watches an enemy army. The ninja counts the soldiers before sneaking away into the dark.

Ninja have existed for hundreds of years. They were most common from the mid-fifteenth century to the seventeenth century when they fought in many wars to control Japan.

The mid-fifteenth century to the seventeenth century in Japan was the Warring States period.

Ninja spied on enemy soldiers.

Ninja were spies and soldiers. They watched the enemy in secret to help plan for battles. Sometimes they fought enemy soldiers.

Ninja received special training to do their jobs. They learned how to spy and attack without ever being noticed.

Ninja worked on strength to surprise their enemy.

Ninja Tales

To be good spies, ninja stayed hidden. During war, their missions were secret. When ninja became less common after the seventeenth century, people spread myths about them.

Some myths said that ninja could fly or that some used magic to kill their enemies.

Other stories told of ninja fighting with special weapons. They used throwing stars. But ninja probably didn't use them to attack.

Ninja used throwing stars to scare their enemy.

Ninja used sickles and other farming tools as weapons.

Real ninja didn't have superpowers. Most of them didn't have special weapons. They used farming tools and swords if they could get them.

Ninja in Action

A farmer meets a group of soldiers on a dusty road. He tells them about an enemy army ahead. But the story is false. The farmer is a ninja in disguise.

Ninja pretended to be farmers.

Ninja had to be sneaky when destroying or stealing supplies.

Ninja told false stories to trick the enemy. They found out where the enemy stored food and other supplies. Then they tried to destroy or steal the supplies.

Ninja dressed to fit in with the people around them. They looked like farmers, soldiers, or miners. They often stayed in disguise for a long time to gain people's trust.

Ninja would blend in to get information.

Ninja would have been noticed if they wore black.

Other times, ninja wore camo clothes. The clothes helped them hide for surprise attacks. Camo colors helped ninja climb castle walls and sneak into enemy camps unseen.

Modern Ninja

Ninja passed their skills on by training new ninja. Some people still learn ninja skills.

Ninja athletes tackle challenging obstacles.

Ninja may be athletes. They jump and climb through a series of obstacles. They race one another for the fastest time.

Some soldiers still fight like ninja. They wear camo. They stay in enemy areas for a long time.

US soldiers do some things that are similar to ninja.

Some soldiers go undercover to learn about their enemy.

Soldiers use ninja skills to help win wars. Ninja soldiers work to keep people safe.

Real-Life Ninja

Fujibayashi Nagato was part of a ninja group called Iga. He served as the leader of Japan's Oomi region in the eighteenth century. Nagato often clashed in battle with followers of famous leader Oda Nobunaga. Nobunaga tried to wipe out Iga, but many ninja escaped.

Before battle, Nagato often prayed for victory at Japan's Tejikara Shrine. The shrine is still popular, and people hold a fireworks festival there each year.

Ninja Fun Facts

- Some myths say ninja can turn invisible. Others tell of ninja wearing all black clothing and masks to hide in the shadows. But most ninja dressed like the people around them.
- Ninja skills and methods are called ninjutsu. Ninjutsu includes fighting styles, ways to be a good spy, and much more.
- The Japanese word for ninja is *shinobi*.

Glossary

camo: colors made to disguise or hide

disguise: clothing used to hide or change one's identity

myth: a story about the past that may not be true

obstacle: something that slows or stops progress

spy: a person who works in secret to gather information

throwing star: a small, sharp weapon used to attack or threaten enemies

Further Reading

Fishman, Jon M. *Train Like a Ninja.* Minneapolis: Lerner Publications, 2020.

Kids Web Japan—Ninja
https://web-japan.org/kidsweb/explore/history/q4.html

Moon, Walt K. *Let's Explore Japan.* Minneapolis: Lerner Publications, 2017.

National Geographic Kids: Japan
https://kids.nationalgeographic.com/explore/countries/japan/

Ninja Facts for Kids
https://kids.kiddle.co/Ninja

Terp, Gail. *Ninja*. Mankato, MN: Black Rabbit Books, 2020.

Index

disguise, 12, 14

Japan, 5

myths, 8-9

soldiers, 4, 6, 12, 14, 18-19

spy, 6, 7, 8

Photo Acknowledgments

Image credits: Gerville/Getty Images, p. 2; Stocktrek Images/Getty Images, p. 4; bedo/Getty Images, p. 5; China Photos/Getty Images, p. 6; Laoshi/Getty Images, p. 7; Kavuto/Getty Images, p. 8; choja/Getty Images, p. 9; Sergii Zysko/Getty Images, p. 10; iEverest/Getty Images, p. 11; John Moore/Getty Images, p. 12; Charissa Van Straalen/EyeEm/Getty Images, p. 13; Katsushika Hokusai. Nakahara in Sagami Province (Soshu Nakahara), 1825-1838. The Art Institute of Chicago, p. 14; NicolasMcComber/Getty Images, p. 15; FatCamera/Getty Images, p. 16; Lorado/Getty Images, p. 17; CAITLIN O'HARA/Getty Images, p. 18; avid_creative/Getty Images, p. 19; volkovslava/Getty Images, p. 22.

Cover: quavondo/Getty Images.

Main body text set in Billy Infant regular. Typeface provided by SparkType.